Gardens Around the Globe:

A COLORING BOOK FOR GROWN-UPS

Sandy Baker

BLACK GARNET PRESS

· SANTA ROSA, CALIFORNIA ·
SANDYBAKERWRITER.COM

Gardens Around the Globe:
A Coloring Book for Grown-ups

Black Garnet Press
P.O. Box 2914
Santa Rosa, CA 95405

To all the grown-ups who still love to color, especially the gardeners.

ISBN 978-0-9911790-4-6

Designed by Rita Ter Sarkissoff • springhillbooks.com • Printed in USA

Also by Sandy Baker

- *Adventures of the Hotel Sisters*, 2015
- *Gai's Go-Away-Come-Back Garden*, 2015
- *Three Sisters Garden*, 2014
- *Howie's Hungabird Dilemma*, 2014
- *Color My Garden* (English and Spanish versions), 2013
- *The Dead Butterflies Diary*, 2013
- *Zack's Zany Zucchiniland*, 2012
- *Mrs. Feeny and the Grubby Garden Gang*, 2011
- *The Tehran Triangle* (with Tom Reed), 2012
- Editor, *The Reagan Enigma: 1964-1980*, by Thomas C. Reed, 2014

See more of Sandy Baker at sandybakerwriter.com

Introduction

We begin at an early age coloring leaves green, tree trunks brown, bricks red, and the sky blue, but it isn't always so. Here's your chance to let your imagination go wild and color these illustrations however you wish, because in your mind's eye, the image could be any color you're seeing or feeling.

Look at any garden and you'll see dozens of shades of green, red, blue, white and yellow. They have exotic names such as vermillion, magenta, indigo, burgundy, maroon, carmine, coral, salmon, fuchsia, goldenrod, khaki, olive, lavender, orchid, lilac, amethyst, chartreuse, foam, lime, aquamarine, turquoise, and many more. Don't you love 'em? Use them. Go crazy!

My illustrations are hand-drawn, referencing photos I've taken over the years during our travels. There's no garden I haven't loved. These are from photographs I took in New Zealand, Guatemala, Germany, France, California, Pennsylvania, Maryland, Virginia, and Washington D.C. You may or may not recognize the places because I've simplified, added, and tweaked so that I could draw them and you could color them.

I hope you enjoy the experience of coloring these images as much as I have enjoyed photographing and illustrating them.

Sandy Baker, April 2017

ACKNOWLEDGEMENT

If it weren't for Rita Ter Sarkissoff, the best friend I've still never met, I wouldn't have published many books. She has been my book and cover designer (and cheerleader) for this and seven others. In the early 2000s, we were UC Sonoma County Master Gardeners together but never ran into each other though we lived only eight or so miles apart. She published the MG newsletter in which she included many of my articles and simple illustrations, but we communicated only by email. We now live more than 650 miles apart, but books keep us working together electronically. I am ever grateful for the outstanding design work Rita does, this adult coloring book being no exception. Many thanks to you, as always, my good friend.

ABOUT THE AUTHOR

Sandy Baker has always loved to draw, having begun as a kid by taking "drawing lessons" from Jon Gnagy in television's early days with his "Learn to Draw" kit. Gnagy died in 1981, but his TV lessons using charcoal pencils and kneaded erasers made an indelible mark on Sandy's creative side. Developing this adult coloring book evolved from her love of gardens and gardening, photography, and drawing. This will be the third book she's illustrated, including the children's *The Dead Butterflies Diary* and *Color My Garden* in English and Spanish. Sandy spent 16 years as a Sonoma County Master Gardener and is currently president of Redwood Writers, the largest of 22 branches in the California Writers Club. Sandy divides her time writing, gardening, reading, and traveling. She lives in Northern California with her husband in a 1924 house whose gardens she's attempting to turn into a mini-Monet scene.

www.ingramcontent.com/pod-product-compliance
Lightning Source LLC
Chambersburg PA
CBHW081637040426
42449CB00014B/3360